WAYNE BARNES:

The Spirit of Rugby: Iconic Legacy of

Wayne Barnes

William E.Davison

TABLE OF CONTENTS

1.2 Instructive foundation of wayne Barnes

1.3 wayne Barnes childhood

1.4 family foundation

1.5 people who is inspired him

8.1 fun reality about

him

CHAPTER 9: HIS

PHILANTHROPISTS

ENDEAVORS

CONCLUSION

INTRODUCTION

Few names in rugby union inspire as much admiration and respect as Wayne Barnes. An incredibly famous ref, Barnes is known for his decency, his position, and his resolute obligation to the soul of the game. In this astute and motivating book, Tony Mercer investigates the qualities that have supported Barnes' famous lifetime, and how he has exemplified the actual substance of what's genuinely going on with rugby.

Mercer follows Barnes' excursion from his initial days as a youthful ref in his local Britain to his ascent to the zenith of the game, directing at probably the greatest matches in rugby history. En route, he digs into the characteristics that have made Barnes so effective, from his fastidious arrangement and meticulousness to his capacity to resist the urge to panic under tension and use wise judgment without giving it much thought.

In any case, something other than a history of a wearing symbol, The Soul of Rugby is a festival of the qualities that lie at the core of the game. On and off the field, Mercer looks at how Barnes has consistently displayed these values of sportsmanship, respect, camaraderie, and integrity. He shows how Barnes has involved his foundation as an official to advance these qualities and rouse others, both inside the rugby local area and then some.

In reality as we know it where the game is frequently discolored by embarrassment and discussion, Wayne Barnes remains as an encouraging sign and respectability. His heritage will be not just as one of the best refs ever, yet in addition as a genuine boss of the soul of rugby.

The Soul of Rugby is a must-peruse for any individual who loves rugby, or who basically values the force of game to advance positive qualities and rouse others.

CHAPTER 1:WHO IS WAYNE BARNES?

Retired English international rugby union referee Wayne Barnes He was one of the most regarded and persuasive arbitrators on the planet, known for his reasonableness, authority, and steadfast obligation to the soul of the game.

Barnes, who was born in 1979, started off as a teenager officiating rugby games. At just 21 years old, he joined the Panel of National Referees and quickly rose through the ranks. He turned into an expert ref in 2005 and made his global presentation in 2006.

Barnes immediately set up a good foundation for himself as one of the world's driving refs. He was well-known for being able to control the game with calm and authoritative demeanor, as well as for his willingness to make difficult choices. He was likewise a fanatic for the standards, which gained him the appreciation of players and mentors the same.

Barnes refereed at the absolute greatest matches in rugby history, including four Rugby World Cups, numerous Six Countries Titles, and a few Heineken Cup finals. He was likewise the principal arbitrator to administer more than 100 Prevalence matches.

Barnes resigned from refereeing in 2019, yet he keeps on being engaged with the game as a reporter and expert. He is also a well-known public speaker who has spoken out in favor of rugby's spirit.

Wayne Barnes is a genuine legend of rugby association. He serves as an example for referees all over the world, and his legacy will continue to inspire players and fans for generations to come.

1.1 Wayne Barnes' early life

Wayne Barnes was born on September 20, 1979, in Bream, Gloucestershire, which is located in the Forest of Dean. He experienced childhood in a common family and went to

Whitecross School, where he succeeded in scholastics and sports. He enjoyed playing tennis and cricket as well as rugby union for the school team. Since early on, Barnes showed a fitness for sports, especially rugby and cricket. He improved his rugby abilities on the fields of Whitecross School, where he went to all through his essential and optional instruction. Regardless of his wearing ability, Barnes never dismissed his scholastics, succeeding in his examinations too.

After finishing his optional training, Barnes left on a regulation degree at the College of East Anglia. His scholastic brightness radiated through, and he graduated with a regulation degree in 2000. With his legal credentials in hand, Barnes pursued a career as a criminal law barrister. His sharp keenness and powerful contentions immediately acquired him acknowledgment in the lawful field.

Running lined up with his lawful profession, Barnes' enthusiasm for rugby refereeing stayed unfaltering. He had taken up refereeing as a youngster and immediately showed a characteristic ability for dealing with the game's complexities. His devotion and reliable improvement prompted his arrangement to the Board of Public Refs in 2001, an exceptional accomplishment at the youthful age of 21.

1.2 instructive foundation of wayne Barnes

Brought into the world in Bream, Gloucestershire, Britain, on September 20, 1979, Wayne Barnes exhibited a strong fascination with scholastics and sports since the beginning. His folks, both working people, imparted in him the upsides of difficult work, determination, and a solid hard working attitude. These qualities would work well for him all through his life, both in his scholar and donning attempts.

Barnes went to Whitecross School, a neighborhood state school in Bream. He succeeded in his examinations, especially in arithmetic and science, and was reliably at the highest point of his group. He was additionally a functioning member in extracurricular exercises, including rugby association, cricket, and tennis.

Barnes' scholastic ability went on all through his auxiliary schooling. He was an industrious and upright understudy, continuously endeavoring to accomplish the most ideal outcomes. His devotion to his investigations paid off, and he procured fantastic grades in his GCSE and A-level assessments.

Barnes went on to study at the University of East Anglia (UEA) in pursuit of a higher education after establishing an impressive academic record at Whitecross School. He decided to concentrate on regulation, a field that intrigued him with its scholarly difficulties and cultural effect. At UEA, Barnes kept on succeeding in his examinations, submerging himself in the complexities of regulation and exhibiting a sharp legitimate psyche.

In 2000, Barnes moved on from UEA with a regulation degree, gaining the appreciation of his companions and teachers. He started a successful career as a lawyer, focusing on criminal law. He quickly gained recognition in the legal field thanks to his strong work ethic, persuasive arguments, and sharp intellect.

While his lawful profession prospered, Barnes never failed to focus on his energy for rugby and his craving to seek after refereeing at the most significant level. He kept on directing at nearby and territorial matches, leveling up his abilities and acquiring important experience. His commitment and ability were clear, and he before long rose through the positions of the rugby refereeing world.

1.3 wayne Barnes childhood

Brought into the world on September 20, 1979, in Bream, Gloucestershire, Britain, Wayne Barnes experienced childhood in a common family with two more seasoned siblings and a more youthful sister. Hard work, perseverance, and a strong work ethic were instilled in him by Alan and Jackie Barnes. He would carry these values with him throughout his life.

Barnes' family resided in an unobtrusive board house in Bream, a little town settled inside the beautiful Backwoods of Senior member. His childhood was filled with love, support, and encouragement from his family, despite the modest surroundings. His parents instilled in him the value of education, honesty, and consideration for others, all of which helped shape his character.

1.4 family foundation

Wayne Barnes was brought into the world on September 20, 1979, in Bream, Gloucestershire, Britain. His folks, Alan and Jackie Barnes, were both working people and raised him and his three kin in an unassuming board house in Bream.

Alan Barnes was a craftsman and Jackie Barnes was a housewife. They instilled strong work ethics, perseverance, and hard work in their children. These qualities would work well for Wayne all through his life. Wayne Barnes experienced childhood in a cherishing and strong family. His folks urged him to seek after his fantasies and never abandon his objectives. They were generally there for him, regardless.

Wayne Barnes has a cozy relationship with his kin. They are all extremely pleased with his achievements. They always look up to him because he serves as a model for them. Wayne Barnes' family is a major piece of his life. . He is exceptionally thankful for their adoration and backing.

1.5 people who is inspired him

Wayne Barnes has refered to a few group as motivations in his day to day existence, both inside the universe of rugby association and then some. The following are a couple of the most outstanding:

His folks, Alan and Jackie Barnes: Wayne's folks imparted in him the upsides of difficult work, steadiness, and respectability, which have been instrumental in his prosperity. They were likewise consistently steady of his enthusiasm for rugby and refereeing.

His rugby trainers: Wayne was lucky to have a few fantastic mentors all through his playing profession, who assisted him with fostering his abilities and comprehension of the game. He attributes his understanding of teamwork, discipline, and respect for the game to them.

His kindred officials: Wayne has consistently respected crafted by other high level officials, and he has advanced an incredible arrangement from them. He is especially thankful for the mentorship and backing of his kindred English arbitrators, like Tony Spreadbury and Derek Bevan

His loved ones: Wayne's better half, Polly, and their two kids have been a steady wellspring of help and consolation all through his profession. He acknowledges them for assisting him with keeping a sound balance between fun and serious activities and to hold his needs under control.

His guides: Wayne has also been fortunate to have mentors outside of the rugby world who have guided and supported him. These incorporate his graduate school teacher, Julian Roberts, and his previous counselor, Geoffrey Cox.

1.6 rising through the ranks

Brought into the world in Bream, Gloucestershire, Britain, in 1979, Wayne Barnes' energy for rugby touched off during his school years. He played for the school group and, at 15 years old, took up refereeing, attracted to the complexities of the game's regulations and the test of keeping everything under control on the field.

His regular ability and devotion immediately grabbed the eye of nearby rugby specialists. Barnes' exhibitions at nearby and provincial matches acquired him acknowledgment for his fair-mindedness, control of the game, and capacity to apply the standards with consistency.

Barnes' great exhibitions at the grassroots level prompted his arrangement to the Board of Public Refs in 2001, a momentous accomplishment early in life of 21. This arrangement opened ways to directing at high level matches, furnishing him with important experience and openness to the most noteworthy echelons of the game.

In 2001, Barnes was appointed to the Panel of National Referees as a result of his impressive performances at the grassroots level—a remarkable accomplishment for a 21-year-old. He gained invaluable experience and exposure to the sport's highest levels as a result of this appointment, which allowed him to officiate at matches of the highest level.

In 2005, Barnes moved forward in his vocation, turning into an expert ref. This noticeable a huge defining moment, permitting him to completely focus on his energy and seek after refereeing at the most significant level.

In 2006, Barnes made his international debut officiating a match between Italy and Romania. This noticeable a crucial second in his profession, moving him onto the worldwide stage and exhibiting his ability to the world.

His exhibitions on the global stage additionally set his standing as one of the world's driving arbitrators. Barnes was known for his quiet disposition, definitive presence, and capacity to settle on difficult choices under tremendous strain.

In 2005, Barnes was appointed to the RFU Elite Referees Academy due to his consistent excellence. He had the chance to improve his skills, learn more about the game, and get ready for the highest level of international competition through this prestigious program.

CHAPTER 2:PREIMER LEAGUE CAREER

Wayne Barnes, the regarded English rugby association arbitrator, never directed in the Head Association, the top division of English football. He devoted his extraordinary profession to the universe of rugby association, where he secured himself as perhaps of the most regarded and powerful arbitrator ever.

Barnes' ascent to noticeable quality in rugby association started very early in life. His energy for the game lighted during his school years, driving him to seek after refereeing at 15 years old. He quickly rose through the ranks of referees thanks to his undying dedication and natural talent, which drew the attention of local rugby authorities.

In 2001, at the astounding age of 21, Barnes was delegated to the Board of Public Arbitrators. This undeniable a huge defining moment in his profession, opening ways to directing at high level coordinates and furnishing him with important experience.

Barnes' devotion to rugby association stayed immovable, and in 2005, he settled on the striking choice to turn proficient. As a result of this decision, he was able to fully devote himself to his passion and work as a referee at the highest level, officiating in prestigious tournaments like the Rugby World Cup, the

European Challenge Cup, and the Heineken Cup.

Barnes' remarkable abilities and unflinching obligation to the soul of rugby acquired him various awards all through his distinguished lifetime. He won the coveted International Rugby Board Referee of the Year award in 2010 and was named Rugby Writers' Club Referee of the Year three times (in 2009, 2013, and 2016).

In 2019, following an unbelievable 18 years of administering at the most significant level, Wayne Barnes chose to resign from refereeing. His inheritance is one of greatness, honesty, and relentless energy for the game. He abandons a void in the realm of rugby, yet his commitments will keep on motivating hopeful refs and rugby lovers around the world.

While Wayne Barnes never directed in the Head Association, his outstanding profession in rugby association fills in as a motivation to people chasing after their interests and succeeding in their picked fields. His devotion, ability, and resolute obligation to the soul of the game are characteristics that resound across every donning discipline.

2.1 Striking matches directed

Wayne Barnes, the eminent English rugby association ref, directed in an exceptional number of prominent matches all through his famous lifetime. His capacity to order the field, keep up with decency, and settle on unequivocal decisions under huge strain gained him the appreciation of players, mentors, and fans around the world. Here is a brief look into some of Wayne Barnes' most remarkable matches directed:

2007 Rugby World Cup Quarter-Last: Britain versus Australia

This exceptionally expected quarter-last match at the 2007 Rugby World Cup in France was a strained and firmly challenged undertaking. Barnes' presentation was generally commended for his control of the game, his treatment of combative minutes, and his capacity to guarantee a fair and cutthroat match.

Final of 2011 Rugby World Cup: The 2011 Rugby World Cup final between New Zealand and France was a significant occasion, and Barnes was given the task of officiating the match. His quiet disposition, legitimate presence, and capacity to apply the standards reliably were instrumental in keeping everything under control and guaranteeing a donning challenge.

Final of 2015 Rugby World Cup: New Zealand versus Australia

One more Rugby World Cup last under Barnes' supervision, the 2015 Rugby World

Cup last at Twickenham Arena in Britain was an undeniably exhilarating experience. In his decision-making and ability to manage the match's high-pressure atmosphere, Barnes demonstrated his expertise and experience.

Final of 2019 Rugby World Cup: Britain versus South Africa

The 2019 Rugby World Cup last in Japan denoted Barnes' third World Cup last arrangement, a demonstration of his uncommon standing and directing abilities. The match was a firmly battled challenge, and Barnes' capacity to keep up with reasonableness and consistency was essential in deciding the result.

Various Six Countries Titles

Barnes was a customary official in the Six Countries Title, the head yearly rugby association rivalry among the six significant European countries. His exhibitions in these matches displayed his authority of the game's standards and his capacity to deal with the power and rawness of the opposition.

Heineken Cup and European Test Cup Finals

Barnes likewise directed in various Heineken Cup and European Test Cup finals, the two significant European club rugby association rivalries. These coordinates gave him a stage to show his skill in high-stakes, high-pressure conditions.

Wayne Barnes' commitments to the universe of rugby association stretch out past these remarkable matches. He has administered in endless other high level experiences, reliably showing his remarkable ability, devotion, and enduring obligation to the soul of the game. His heritage as perhaps of the most regarded and persuasive arbitrator in rugby history is immovably established.

2.2 On-Field Accomplishments

Administered at four Rugby World Cups (2007, 2011, 2015, 2019)

Barnes' attendance at four Rugby World Cups, the zenith of the game, is a demonstration of his excellent abilities and notoriety. He has directed in the absolute most essential matches in World Cup history, including the 2007 Quarter-Last among Britain and Australia, the 2011 Last between New Zealand and France, the 2015 Last between New Zealand and Australia, and the 2019 Last among Britain and South Africa.

Referred at multiple Six Nations Championships The premier annual rugby union competition between the six major European nations is the Six Nations Championship. Barnes' ordinary cooperation in this lofty competition features his dominance of the game's standards and his capacity to deal with the extraordinary and actual nature of the opposition.

Directed in Heineken Cup and European Test Cup Finals

The Heineken Cup and European Test Cup are the two significant European club rugby association rivalries. Barnes' contribution in the finals of these competitions grandstands his skill in high-stakes, high-pressure conditions.

2.3 His Awards

Rugby Authors' Club Arbitrator of the Year (2009, 2013, 2016)

The Rugby Journalists' Club Ref of the Year grant is a profoundly desired acknowledgment presented to the ref who has exhibited uncommon execution and commitment to the game. Barnes' three-time receipt of this grant says a lot of his predictable greatness and effect on the game.

Worldwide Rugby Board Arbitrator of the Year (2010)

The Global Rugby Board Arbitrator of the Year grant is the apex of acknowledgement for refs in the realm of rugby association. Barnes' determination as the top official in 2010 highlights his worldwide standing and the regard he orders from the rugby local area.

Extra Acknowledgment

Barnes has gotten various different honors all through his profession, including the BBC Sports Character Arbitrator of the Year grant, the Rugby Players' Affiliation Unique Legitimacy Grant, and the RFU President's Honor. His legacy as one of rugby's most distinguished referees is further strengthened by these awards.

Past the Field

Wayne Barnes' effect stretches out past the rugby field. He is a regarded public speaker and has been vocal in advancing the upsides of rugby, like sportsmanship, regard, fellowship, and trustworthiness. In addition, he is actively involved in mentoring and inspiring aspiring referees, imparting his expertise and guiding them in their pursuit of their passion for the sport.

CHAPTER 3: INTERNATIONAL CAREER

Wayne Barnes, the regarded English rugby association arbitrator, has carved his name into the archives of rugby history as perhaps of the most regarded and powerful figure in the game. His global vocation, spreading over 17 years and including four Rugby World Cups, is a demonstration of his uncommon ability, immovable devotion, and unflinching obligation to the soul of rugby.

In 2006, Barnes made his international debut officiating a match between Italy and Romania. This noticeable a crucial second in his profession, moving him onto the worldwide stage and exhibiting his ability to the world.

Barnes' exhibitions on the global stage additionally set his standing as one of the world's driving arbitrators. Barnes' international career was unquestionably defined by his participation in four Rugby World Cups—2007, 2011, 2015, and 2019—which earned him the respect of players, coaches, and fans alike. He was known for his calm demeanor, authoritative presence, and capacity to make difficult decisions under tremendous pressure. His attendance at the zenith of the game is a demonstration of his uncommon abilities and notoriety.

The highly competitive and high-stakes quarterfinal match between England and Australia in 2007 was officiated by Barnes. His presentation was broadly lauded for his control of the game, his treatment of quarrelsome minutes, and his capacity to guarantee a fair and serious match.

Barnes' standing proceeded to develop, and in 2011, he was depended with the obligation of administering the Rugby World Cup last between New Zealand and France. Barnes' decision-making and ability to manage the match's high-pressure atmosphere demonstrated his expertise and experience in a tense and close contest.

After four years, Barnes was chosen once more to officiate the Rugby World Cup final between Australia and New Zealand. The match was one more exciting experience, and Barnes' capacity to keep up with reasonableness and consistency was urgent in deciding the result.

In 2019, Barnes' distinguished global vocation finished with his arrangement to administer at his third World Cup last, this time among Britain and South Africa. The match was a close one, and Barnes' ability to be fair and consistent played a big role in deciding the outcome once more.

Past the Rugby World Cups, Barnes administered in various other high level global matches, including Six Countries Titles, Heineken Cup finals, and European Test Cup finals. His predictable greatness on the global stage procured him further acknowledgment, including the BBC Sports Character Arbitrator of the Year grant and the Rugby Players' Affiliation Unique Legitimacy Grant.

The international career of Wayne Barnes is notable in the history of rugby refereeing. Players, coaches, fans, and the wider rugby community worldwide respect him for his exceptional talent, unwavering dedication, and dedication to the spirit of rugby.

Barnes' heritage reaches out past the awards and acknowledgment. He has enlivened incalculable hopeful arbitrators through his mentorship and direction, sharing his insight and experience to assist them with fostering their abilities and seek after their enthusiasm for the game.

As Wayne Barnes considers his celebrated worldwide profession, he can do as such with monstrous pride and fulfillment. He has succeeded as a ref as well as filled in as a representative for the game, advancing its qualities and motivating people in the future of rugby fans.

3.1 FIFA affirmation

Wayne Barnes isn't a FIFA ensured ref, nor has he at any point directed in any

FIFA-endorsed matches. His vocation has been solely centered around rugby association, where he has secured himself as quite possibly of the most regarded and compelling figure in the game.

Barnes' mastery lies in the unpredictable standards and subtleties of rugby association, which contrast altogether from the Laws of the Game that administer affiliation football. While the two games share a shared objective of keeping up with reasonableness and request on the field, the particular standards and translations shift impressively.

To turn into a FIFA-guaranteed official, people should go through thorough preparation and evaluation processes well defined for affiliation football. This incorporates understanding the Laws of the Game, breezing through wellness assessments, and exhibiting capability in different parts of administering, for example, situating, navigation, and correspondence.

Wayne Barnes' emphasis on rugby association has permitted him to foster a profound comprehension of the game and its interesting difficulties. His commitment to rugby association has procured him various honors, including three Rugby Authors' Club Ref of the Year grants and the sought after Global Rugby Board Ref of the Year grant in 2010.

CHAPTER 4: HIS SHORTCOMINGS

Wayne Barnes is broadly viewed as one of the best rugby arbitrators ever, however even the most excellent competitors and authorities have their deficiencies. Although Barnes' advantages far outweigh his disadvantages, it is essential to acknowledge the areas in which he could have done better.

Decision-making that is not always consistent: Barnes, similar to any human authority, was helpless to periodic blunders in judgment. There were occurrences where his choices were addressed, especially in high-pressure circumstances.

Correspondence might have been more clear: Now and again, Barnes' correspondence with players and mentors might have been more straightforward and itemized. His decisions might have been less frustrating and misunderstood if he had provided more precise explanations.

Overseeing scrum encroachments: In rugby, scrum infractions are a common problem, and Barnes' handling of these incidents could have been better. Distinguishing and punishing encroachments successfully is pivotal for keeping up with fair play.

Making adjustments to new rules: The guidelines of rugby are continually advancing, and Barnes at times attempted to speedily adjust to new guidelines. Staying aware of the most recent changes and applying them reliably was significant for keeping up with reasonableness.

Dealing with the close to home force of matches: Rugby is an enthusiastic and sincerely charged sport, and Barnes might have worked on his capacity to deal with the power of certain matches. Staying cool headed and settling on quiet choices under enormous strain is fundamental for a high level ref.

Regardless of these weaknesses, Wayne
Barnes' commitments to rugby association
are irrefutable. His devotion, mastery, and
resolute obligation to the game have gained
him the appreciation of players, mentors,
fans, and the more extensive rugby local area.
His heritage as perhaps the most recognized
arbitrator in rugby history is solidly
solidified.

4.1 how he conquered his shortcomings

Wayne Barnes, broadly viewed as one of the
best rugby refs ever, persistently strived to
work on all through his famous lifetime.
While his assets far offset his weaknesses, he
perceived regions where he could improve

his administering abilities. This is the way Barnes tended to and defeated a portion of his apparent weaknesses:

erratic decision-making: In order to identify patterns in his decision-making, Barnes actively sought feedback from teammates, coaches, and analysts. He carefully analyzed his calls and match footage, paying close attention to contentious situations and decisions that were borderline. He was able to refine his decision-making criteria and pinpoint areas for improvement through this process of self-evaluation.

Muddled correspondence: Barnes perceived the significance of clear and brief correspondence with players and mentors. In order to improve his ability to articulate his decisions and justify them, he discussed them with seasoned referees and communication experts. He additionally rehearsed his relational abilities in reproduced match situations, guaranteeing that his clarifications were clear, direct, and deferential.

Overseeing scrum encroachments: Barnes devoted additional chance to concentrating on the complexities of scrum guidelines and examining late patterns in scrum encroachments. He looked for direction from scrum subject matter experts and working on recognizing and punishing encroachments during instructional meetings. This emphasis on scrum directing brought about a more predictable and successful way to deal with dealing with these vital parts of the game.

Adjusting to new guidelines: Barnes made a conscious effort to keep up with the most recent rugby union rule changes. He consistently evaluated the refreshed Laws of the Game, went to courses and studios directed by rugby specialists, and looked for explanation from individual refs and specialists on any ambiguities or intricacies. This obligation to staying aware of the advancing guidelines guaranteed that his directing stayed reliable and lined up with the most recent guidelines.

Managing one's emotions: Under the intense pressure of high-stakes matches, Barnes was aware of the need to maintain control and composure. He rehearsed care methods, participated in mental preparation works out, and looked for guidance from sports analysts to foster profound guideline abilities. He likewise submerged himself in the investigation of match brain science, grasping the profound elements of players, mentors, and observers. This emphasis on profound administration assisted him with trying to avoid panicking, unequivocal, and in control even in the most genuinely charged circumstances.

Wayne Barnes' eagerness to address his deficiencies and consistently take a stab at progress is a demonstration of his devotion to greatness and his faithful obligation to the game of rugby association. His efforts to improve his communication skills, manage the emotional intensity of matches, and improve his officiating abilities all contributed to his improved performance and solidified his status as one of the greatest referees of all time.

CHAPTER 5:REFEREEING STYLE

Wayne Barnes' style of refereeing was distinguished by his calm demeanor, authoritative presence, and capacity to make decisive decisions under tremendous pressure. He was known for his severe adherence to the principles, his capacity to keep up with control of the game, and his fair and predictable way to deal with navigation.

Key Components of Wayne Barnes' Refereeing Style:

Composed and tranquil: Barnes had an ability to outstanding to stay cool and created under extreme strain. He never permitted the feelings of the game to impact his choices, guaranteeing that his directing stayed fair-minded and objective.

Influential Presence: Barnes deserved admiration on the field with his definitive presence. His sure attitude and clear correspondence guaranteed that players and mentors grasped his choices and regarded his position.

Making decisive choices: Barnes was famous for being able to make quick, decisive decisions under a lot of pressure. He had a profound comprehension of the standards and could apply them reliably, even in the most perplexing and hostile circumstances.

Severe Adherence to Rules: Barnes was a severe disciple to the principles of the game, guaranteeing that fair play was kept up with all through the match. He wouldn't hesitate to punish encroachments, regardless of whether they came from headliners or groups.

Fair and Steady Methodology: Barnes' direction was portrayed by decency and consistency. He applied the standards consistently, no matter what the group or the circumstance. This decency gained him the appreciation of players, mentors, and fans the same.

Notwithstanding these key components, Barnes was additionally known for his great relational abilities, his capacity to deal with the profound power of matches, and his capacity to adjust to various playing styles and conditions. His refereeing style was a model for hopeful officials all over the planet.

5.1 relational abilities

Wayne Barnes, the regarded English rugby association ref, was broadly viewed as an expert of correspondence on the field. His success as a referee was largely due to his capacity to communicate clearly and concisely with players, coaches, and spectators as well as to articulate his decisions and the reasons behind them.

Important Characteristics of Wayne Barnes'
Communication Skills:

Simple, Clear Language: Barnes utilized
clear and brief language while speaking with
players and mentors. He tried not to involve
specialized language and made sense of his
choices in a clear way, guaranteeing that
everybody figured out the reasoning behind
his calls.

Clarified Explanations: Barnes was renowned
for his ability to effectively communicate his
decisions. He gave clear clarifications of the
principles that had been encroached and the
results of those encroachments. This
clearness assisted with decreasing

disappointment and errors among players and mentors.

Undivided attention: Barnes was an attentive person, cautiously taking into account the worries and clarifications of players and mentors. He esteemed open correspondence and tried to grasp their points of view, even in disagreeable circumstances.

Conscious Tone: Barnes kept a deferential tone in his correspondence, in any event, while managing warmed or close to home circumstances. He tended to players and mentors by name, stayed away from accusatory language, and zeroed in on settling issues cooperatively.

Communication without speaking: Barnes really used non-verbal correspondence signs to enhance his verbal cooperations. His non-verbal communication, looks, and hand signals conveyed his position, certainty, and capacity to control the game.

Barnes' relational abilities were not restricted to verbal trades. He utilized his situating on the field to convey his choices outwardly, guaranteeing that players and observers knew about his calls. He additionally kept up with open correspondence with his touch judges, teaming up successfully to deal with the match.

Wayne Barnes' capacity to impart really was a vital component of his prosperity as a ref.

His reasonable, succinct, and conscious way to deal with correspondence assisted with keeping everything under control, decrease errors, and encourage a positive climate on the field. His relational abilities filled in as a model for hopeful refs and keep on being respected by rugby fans around the world.

5.2 physical wellness

Wayne Barnes was known for his extraordinary actual wellness all through his refereeing profession. The requests of rugby refereeing are tremendous, expecting refs to keep an elevated degree of perseverance, deftness, and solidarity to stay aware of the high speed and genuinely requesting nature of the game. Barnes devoted himself to keeping up with his actual wellness, guaranteeing that he could perform at his best on the field.

Key Parts of Wayne Barnes' Actual Wellness:

Endurance: Barnes had outstanding perseverance, permitting him to keep up with a similar degree of execution all through a whole match. He could run consistently for significant stretches, keeping up with his situating and settling on fast choices without tiring.

Agility: Barnes' dexterity was vital for exploring the jam-packed field and remaining nearby the play. He could take an alternate route rapidly, keep away from impacts, and position himself really to settle on exact decisions.

Strength: Barnes' solidarity was obvious in his capacity to keep up with control in scrums, breakdowns, and other actual showdowns. He could draw in with players of all sizes and handle the rawness of the game with certainty.

Preparing Schedule: Barnes kept a thorough preparation routine to keep up with his actual wellness. He integrated different types of activity, including running, swimming, rec center exercises, and yoga, to foster all parts of his practical preparation.

Actual Arrangement: Barnes painstakingly ready for each match, guaranteeing that he was actually prepared for the requests of the game. He fitted his preparation and sustenance to the particular necessities of the match, taking into account factors like the climate, the resistance, and the style of play.

Barnes' uncommon actual wellness was a demonstration of his devotion to his art. It permitted him to perform at the most elevated level for a lengthy period, directing in the absolute most esteemed matches in the realm of rugby association.

5.3 Decision-making

Wayne Barnes was renowned for his exceptional decision-making abilities, which were a key component of his success as a rugby union referee. His dedication to physical fitness serves as an inspiration to aspiring athletes and referees worldwide. His capacity to make fast, conclusive, and precise calls under tremendous tension gained him the appreciation of players, mentors, and fans around the world.

The Following Factors Influence Wayne Barnes' Excellent Decision-Making:

Profound Comprehension of the Principles: Barnes had a profound comprehension of the complex and consistently developing Laws of the Game. He was continually concentrating on the guidelines, going to instructional meetings, and looking for direction from experienced refs to guarantee that his insight stayed exceptional.

Capacity to Survey Circumstances Rapidly: Barnes had an excellent capacity to evaluate circumstances rapidly and precisely, even in the most turbulent and speedy minutes on the field. He could distinguish encroachments, decide their seriousness, and apply the principles reliably.

Staying cool headed Under Tension: Even when he had to deal with contentious situations or matches that were filled with a lot of emotion, Barnes remained cool and collected under a lot of pressure. His capacity to stay cool headed permitted him to pursue evenhanded and fair-minded choices.

Experience and Versatility: Barnes' broad involvement with refereeing at the most significant level gave him priceless experiences and senses. He could expect likely encroachments, adjust to various playing styles, and pursue choices that kept the game fair and cutthroat.

Correspondence and Counsel: Barnes improved his decision-making process by utilizing consultation and communication effectively. He discussed obviously with his touch judges, looking for their contribution on basic calls, and utilized his relational abilities to actually deal with the game.

Barnes' extraordinary critical thinking abilities were not restricted to explicit circumstances or sorts of encroachments. He was similarly adroit at taking care of scrums, breakdowns, offside calls, and other complex parts of the game. His capacity to make fast, unequivocal, and exact calls under tension was a principal quality of his refereeing style.

5.4 relationship with players

Wayne Barnes was known for his aware and proficient connection with players all through his famous refereeing profession. He maintained a positive rapport with players, both on and off the field, and commanded respect on the field with his authority and fairness.

Key Parts of Wayne Barnes' Relationship with Players:

Respectful Attitude: Barnes approached players with deference, in any event, while managing disagreeable circumstances or punishing encroachments. He greeted each player by name, paid close attention to their concerns, and conducted himself with respect at all times.

Open Correspondence: With players, Barnes valued open communication and sought to comprehend their perspectives and clearly explain his decisions. He was approachable, which helped him build a good working relationship with the players.

Fair and Steady Methodology: Barnes' decency and consistency in applying the principles gained him the appreciation of players. He treated all players similarly, no matter what their standing or group association.

Positive Input: Barnes made use of positive player feedback to improve his refereeing. He discussed openly with other players to learn more about their decision-making and communication abilities.

Off-field Cooperations: Barnes kept up with positive associations with players off the field, showing that he esteemed their perspectives and regarded their commitments to the game. He went to player occasions, participated in friendly communications, and constructed compatibility with players as people.

Barnes' relationship with players was not exclusively founded on shared regard. He likewise had a profound comprehension of the game and the tensions that players face. He could expect their activities, evaluate their goals, and pursue choices that guaranteed the wellbeing and decency of the game for all players.

Wayne Barnes' way to deal with player connections set an elevated expectation for trying refs. His success as a referee was significantly influenced by his capacity to command respect, maintain open communication, and treat players fairly and professionally. His inheritance isn't just characterized by his outstanding thinking abilities yet additionally by his capacity to cultivate positive associations with players, mentors, and fans the same.

5.5 relationship with managers

Wayne Barnes was exceptionally respected for his capacity to keep up with positive and expert associations with rugby association directors all through his distinguished lifetime. His quiet disposition, legitimate presence, and devotion to fair play gained him the appreciation of mentors, even in the most extraordinary and serious conditions.

Key Parts of Wayne Barnes' Relationship with Supervisors:

Conscious Collaborations: Barnes approached directors with deference, in any event, while managing conflicts or antagonistic choices. He avoided using accusatory language, clarified his decisions, and listened intently to their concerns.

Open Correspondence: With managers, Barnes valued open communication and sought to comprehend their perspectives and clearly articulate his decisions. He took part in customary conversations with mentors, giving criticism and looking for their contribution on keeping up with fair play and game administration.

Consistency and Consistency: Managers trusted Barnes because of his consistent and predictable approach to officiating. They realize that he would apply the principles reasonably and unbiasedly, no matter what the group or circumstance.

Tending to Worries Proactively: Barnes looked to address supervisors' interests proactively, expecting likely issues and imparting his expectations plainly. This proactive methodology assisted with staying away from false impressions and keep a positive working relationship with mentors.

Regard for the Game: Barnes shared a typical regard for the sport of rugby association with chiefs. He comprehended their enthusiasm for their groups and their craving to win, while likewise maintaining the upsides of fair play and sportsmanship.

Barnes' capacity to keep up with positive associations with administrators was not just about overseeing characters. He likewise had a profound comprehension of the game's strategies, techniques, and the tensions looked by mentors. He could expect to mentor choices, evaluate possible struggles, and settle on choices that guaranteed the respectability and intensity of the match.

CHAPTER 6: IMPACT ON THE GAME

Wayne Barnes, the regarded English rugby association ref, has made a permanent imprint on the game, affecting its direction and molding its principles of administering through his extraordinary ability, faithful devotion, and immovable obligation to the soul of rugby.

Raising the Principles of Administering

Barnes' effect on rugby association is most obvious in his height of refereeing principles. He set a new standard for referees worldwide with his calm demeanor, authoritative presence, and capacity to make decisive decisions under extreme pressure. His reliable use of the guidelines, paying little mind to group or circumstance, imparted trust in players, mentors, and fans, cultivating a feeling of decency and respectability inside the game.

Motivating Hopeful Refs

Barnes' impact stretched out past the field, rousing incalculable hopeful arbitrators to seek after their energy for the game. His devotion to personal development, his eagerness to share his insight, and his mentorship of more youthful arbitrators have enhanced the administering local area and guaranteed the continuation of excellent directing in rugby association.

Promoting Rugby's Values Barnes had an impact that went beyond the specifics of refereeing. He exemplified the upsides of rugby - sportsmanship, regard, brotherhood, and uprightness - both on and off the field. His lead, his connections with players and mentors, and his commitment to fair play filled in as a model for all members in the game, building up its extraordinary culture and customs.

Recognition on a Global Scale Barnes' contributions to rugby union have been acknowledged on a global scale. His various honors, including the Worldwide Rugby

Board Arbitrator of the Year grant and three Rugby Essayists' Club Ref of the Year grants, stand as demonstrations of his remarkable abilities and faithful obligation to the game.

Past the honors, Barnes' heritage lies in the positive effect he has had on the game's general trustworthiness, the advancement of trying refs, and the advancement of its qualities. His name is associated with exceptional officiating, and he will continue to have an impact on rugby union for future generations.

6.1 influence on other referees

The impact that Wayne Barnes has had on the other referees has been profound and extensive. His remarkable ability, enduring devotion, and relentless obligation to the soul of rugby have set another benchmark for refs around the world, motivating innumerable people to seek after their enthusiasm for the game and raising the principles of directing across all degrees of rugby association.

Hopeful Officials and Coaching

Barnes has been instrumental in coaching and directing yearning arbitrators, sharing his insight, experience, and bits of knowledge to assist them with fostering their abilities and seek after their enthusiasm for administering. His readiness to draw in with more youthful arbitrators, give productive criticism, and exhibit the significance of constant personal growth has been instrumental in forming the up and coming age of rugby association refs.

Setting New Standards Barnes has set a new standard for referees worldwide with his exceptional decision-making abilities, calm demeanor, authoritative presence, and consistent application of the rules. His capacity to settle on conclusive decisions under monstrous tension, keep up with control of the game, and guarantee fair play has motivated hopeful refs to imitate his methodology and take a stab at the best expectations of directing.

Advancing Qualities and Morals

Past specialized abilities, Barnes has imparted in hopeful arbitrators the significance of maintaining the upsides of rugby - sportsmanship, regard, kinship, and honesty. His lead on and off the field, his connections with players and mentors, and his enduring obligation to fair play have filled in as a model for refs, underscoring the moral rules that support the game.

6.2 future possibilities

Wayne Barnes formally resigned from rugby association refereeing in 2019 following a wonderful 17-year profession at the most elevated level. His retirement denoted the conclusion of a significant time period, as he was generally viewed as quite possibly the most regarded and persuasive arbitrator in rugby history. Nonetheless, Barnes' commitments to the game keep on being felt, and his future possibilities are brilliant as he leaves on new undertakings.

Expected Jobs in Rugby Association

Notwithstanding his retirement from dynamic refereeing, Barnes remains profoundly associated with the game and is probably going to keep assuming a huge part in its turn of events. His reputation, experience, and expertise could be put to use in a variety of ways, including:

Refereeing Tutor and Teacher: Barnes' broad information and bits of knowledge could be important in coaching and teaching yearning arbitrators. He could share his encounters, give direction on navigation, and assist with fostering the up and coming age of high level refs.

Rugby Association Expert and Reporter: Barnes' sharp comprehension of the game's principles, strategies, and systems could make him a sought-after examiner and reporter. His bits of knowledge could give significant viewpoints to fans and news sources, upgrading how they might interpret the game.

Rugby Association Minister and Promoter: Barnes's fame and charisma could be used to advance rugby union's ideals. He could act as a minister for the game, drawing in with fans, schools, and networks to motivate support and energy for the game. .

6.3 Past Rugby Association

Barnes' abilities and experience stretch out past the rugby field. His capacity to oversee complex circumstances, settle on speedy choices under tension, and impart really could be important in different fields, including:

Administration and The Executives Expert: Barnes could be a sought-after consultant in sports, business, and other organizations due to his leadership qualities, decision-making abilities, and ability to handle complicated situations.

Compromise and Intervention: Barnes' capacity to try to avoid panicking under tension, listen mindfully, and figure out something worth agreeing on could be significant in compromise and intercession jobs.

Public Talking and Inspirational orator: Barnes' mystique, relational abilities, and helpful story could make him an effective public speaker and persuasive orator, imparting his encounters and experiences to crowds around the world.

Wayne Barnes' future possibilities are without a doubt brilliant. His devotion to rugby association, his outstanding abilities, and his different encounters position him well for progress in different undertakings. Whether he decides to remain effectively engaged with rugby or adventure into new fields, his commitments will keep on being felt, and his inheritance will persevere.

CHAPTER 7: HIS RETIREMENT

Wayne Barnes' retirement from rugby association refereeing in 2019 denoted the conclusion of a significant time period and the takeoff of perhaps of the most regarded and powerful figure in the game. His distinguished lifetime, spreading over 17 years at the most significant level, was described by outstanding ability, immovable devotion, and a relentless obligation to the soul of rugby.

A Wonderful Vocation

Barnes' heritage is solidly solidified in the archives of rugby history. He administered in north of 200 top of the line matches, including different World Cups, Six Countries competitions, and European Cup finals. His capacity to make fast, conclusive, and precise calls under tremendous tension gained him the appreciation of players, mentors, and fans around the world.

Barnes' effect reached out past his on-field exhibitions. He was a good example for yearning officials, sharing his insight and experience through tutoring and training programs. He additionally supported fair play and respectability, maintaining the qualities that support the game of rugby.

Retirement and Then some

In spite of his retirement from dynamic refereeing, Barnes remains profoundly associated with the game and keeps on making critical commitments. He fills in as a guide and counsel hoping for refs, sharing his experiences and mastery to assist them with fostering their abilities and arrive at their maximum capacity.

Barnes likewise participates in different talking commitment, offering his encounters and points of view to crowds around the world. He is a sought-after examiner and observer for rugby communicates, giving significant bits of knowledge into the game's standards, strategies, and procedures.

Also, Barnes' impact stretches out past rugby association. His authority characteristics, thinking abilities, and capacity to oversee complex circumstances have made him a sought-after expert in different fields, including business, sports, and compromise.

A Tradition of Greatness

Wayne Barnes' heritage is one of greatness, uprightness, and devotion to the game of rugby association. His uncommon ability, unfaltering responsibility, and positive effect have made a permanent imprint on the game, molding its guidelines of administering and moving innumerable people to seek after their enthusiasm for rugby.

Barnes' commitments reach out past the specialized parts of refereeing. He has imparted in refs and players the same the significance of maintaining the upsides of rugby - sportsmanship, regard, brotherhood, and trustworthiness. His lead on and off the field has filled in as a model for all members in the game, supporting its exceptional culture and customs.

Wayne Barnes' retirement denoted the conclusion of a significant time period, however his heritage keeps on living on. His impact on the game is certain, and his commitments will keep on being felt for a long time into the future. He stays a motivation to hopeful refs and a regarded figure in the realm of rugby association.

CHAPTER 8: PERSONAL LIFE

Wayne Barnes, the regarded English rugby association ref, has kept a somewhat confidential individual life, keeping his family and individual matters to a great extent out of the public eye. However, glimpses into his personal life show his love for activities outside of rugby and his devotion to his family.

Family Life: Polly Barnes and Barnes are married and have two children together. He is known to be a given spouse and father, focusing on his family time in spite of his requesting vocation as a ref. His better half, Polly, has been an immovable ally all through his profession, going with him to competitions and offering consolation and backing.

Passion for Music Barnes has a passion for music in addition to rugby union. He is a self-educated guitarist and appreciates playing in groups and going to shows. He uses music as a creative outlet, which enables him to unwind and express himself in a new way.

Interest in Writing

Barnes is additionally an ardent peruser, especially appreciating verifiable fiction and memoirs. Perusing permits him to grow his insight, investigate alternate points of view, and loosen up from the requests of his expert life.

Obligation to Local area

Barnes is effectively associated with his local area, supporting different causes and associations. He is especially energetic about advancing rugby among youngsters and empowering them to embrace sound and dynamic ways of life.

A Healthy lifestyle

While Barnes is without a doubt devoted to rugby association, he has likewise developed a satisfying individual life that gives equilibrium and satisfaction. His obligation to his family, his energy for music and writing, and his contribution locally exhibit his capacity to keep a balanced life past his expert accomplishments.

Wayne Barnes' own life mirrors his qualities and needs. His commitment to his family, pursuit of personal interests, and giving back to the community demonstrate his well-rounded character and capacity for happiness and fulfillment outside of the rugby field.

8.1 fun reality about him

Beside being an uncommon rugby association ref, Wayne Barnes is additionally known for his speedy mind and awareness of what's actually funny. The following are a couple of fun realities about him:

Melodic Ability: Barnes is a self-trained guitarist and appreciates playing in groups and going to shows. His melodic advantages range from rock and blues to traditional and people.

Love of Literature: Barnes reads a lot, especially historical fiction and biographies. He has communicated reverence for creators like Bernard Cornwell and Winston Churchill.

Local area Commitment: Barnes is effectively associated with his local area, supporting different foundations and associations, especially those advancing rugby among youngsters and sound ways of life.

Humble Character: Regardless of his surprising accomplishments, Barnes stays humble and grounded. He is known for his sensible nature and eagerness to interface with fans and yearning officials.

Family Man: Barnes is a committed spouse and father. He cherishes family time and his wife Polly and their two children's support.

Comical inclination: Barnes is known for his speedy mind and funny bone, frequently utilizing his carefree way to deal with ease pressure and interface with others.

Non-Rugby Interests: Barnes partakes in various exercises past rugby, including climbing, cycling, and investing energy outside. He likewise has an enthusiasm for cooking and attempting new foods.

Retirement Plans: Barnes has communicated interest in chasing after a lifelong in communicating or sports news coverage, utilizing his insight and involvement with the rugby world.

Legacy: Barnes' effect on rugby association stretches out past his on-field exhibitions. He has tutored innumerable hopeful arbitrators and advocated fair play, making a permanent imprint on the game's way of life and principles.

Good example: Barnes is broadly regarded for his devotion, respectability, and obligation to the upsides of rugby association. He fills in as a good example for hopeful officials and rugby fans around the world.

CHAPTER 9: HIS PHILANTHROPISTS ENDEAVORS

All through his famous lifetime, Wayne Barnes has exhibited a profound obligation to rewarding the local area and supporting different humanitarian undertakings. His energy for rugby association stretched out past the field, as he perceived the game's capability to rouse, engage, and change lives.

Advancing Rugby Among Youngsters

Barnes put stock in the groundbreaking force of rugby association and its capacity to impart significant life illustrations in youngsters. He actively supported initiatives that provided access to equipment, coaching, and mentorship to underserved communities in order to introduce rugby. His objective was to encourage an affection for the game and advance its positive effect on youth improvement.

Upholding for Wellbeing and Prosperity

Barnes perceived the significance of actual work and solid ways of life for generally speaking prosperity. He gave his support to organizations that helped families and children develop healthy habits by encouraging sports, nutrition education, and active lifestyles. His point was to engage people to settle on informed decisions and focus on their wellbeing.

Supporting Foundations and Causes

Barnes loaned his time and assets to different foundations and causes that lined up with his qualities. He upheld associations zeroed in on schooling, neediness mitigation, and handicap support. His commitments reached out past monetary gifts, as he effectively took part in gathering pledges occasions, chipped in his time, and brought issues to light for these significant causes.

Tutoring and Motivating Hopeful Officials

Barnes perceived the force of tutoring and direction in molding the up and coming age of rugby association arbitrators. He devoted his time and mastery coaching yearning for refs, sharing his insight, encounters, and experiences. His objective was to raise the principles of directing and sustain an energy for the game's respectability.

Advancing Fair Play and Sportsmanship

Barnes epitomized the upsides of fair play and sportsmanship both on and off the field. Through his actions, words, and mentoring, he stood up for these principles. He ensured that all players were treated fairly and with respect and urged referees to uphold the highest standards of officiating.

Wayne Barnes' generous endeavors were not simple motions; they mirrored his firmly established faith in the force of game to change lives and have a beneficial outcome on society. His devotion to offering in return and advancing positive change set his heritage as a genuine good example, in the realm of rugby association as well as a philanthropic and advocate for a superior world.

CONCLUSION

Wayne Barnes' inheritance reaches out a long ways past the rugby field. His resolute obligation to fair play, his remarkable thinking abilities, and his capacity to stay cool headed under monstrous tension have gained him the appreciation of players, mentors, and fans around the world. In any case, his effect on the game is much more significant than that. Barnes has worked tirelessly to promote the sportsmanship, respect, camaraderie, and integrity of rugby. He has utilized his foundation to elevate these qualities and to move youngsters to embrace them.

Mentorship and direction are also left behind by Barnes. He has magnanimously imparted his insight and experience desiring refs, assisting them with fostering their abilities and to arrive at their maximum capacity. He has likewise been a vocal ally of drives that advance rugby among youngsters, especially those from underserved networks.

Although Barnes's time as an active referee is over, his legacy will continue. He is a motivation to hopeful refs and a regarded figure in the realm of rugby association. His story is a demonstration of the force of difficult work, commitment, and honesty.

Printed in Great Britain
by Amazon

34324872R00066